THE LIBRARY OF WEAPONS OF MASS DESTRUCTION™

Chemical *and* Biological Weapons *in a* Post-9/11 World

JANELL BROYLES

The Rosen Publishing Group, Inc., New York

Published in 2005 by The Rosen Publishing Group, Inc.
29 East 21st Street, New York, NY 10010

First Edition

Library of Congress Cataloging-in-Publication

Broyles, Janell.

Chemical and biological weapons in a post-9/11 world / by Janell Broyles.
   p. cm. — (Library of weapons of mass destruction)
ISBN 1-4042-0288-9 (library binding)
1. Chemical warfare—Juvenile literature. 2. Chemical terrorism—Juvenile literature. 3. Biological warfare—Juvenile literature. 4. Bioterrorism—Prevention—United States—Juvenile literature. 5. War on Terrorism, 2001—Juvenile literature.
I. Title. II. Series.

UG447.B744 2005

358'.34—dc22

2004015138

Manufactured in the United States of America

On the cover: Rescue workers practice transporting victims to a decontaminated area in a simulated biohazard exercise in Illinois.

[CONTENTS]

INTRODUCTION

U ntil the twentieth century, people usually thought of warfare as soldiers fighting each other with weapons. Over time, the weapons changed from spears and arrows to cannons and guns. But soldiers still remained the most important element in warfare. Much of the time, it was soldiers who took the risks and did the fighting, not ordinary people—not civilians.

In the late nineteenth and early twentieth centuries, scientists began to make discoveries about how diseases spread and affected the body.

Here, a firefighter shows how to wash down a person contaminated with chemical or biological materials. This drill, conducted at Los Angeles International Airport, was an effort to demonstrate the specialized equipment Los Angeles firefighters would utilize in case of an attack. The 9/11 attacks prompted numerous safety measures such as this in international airports across the country.

Scientists also learned more about how to mix chemicals in new and more powerful ways. These new discoveries and new technologies led to the creation of weapons that could kill many more people more quickly than ever before. In fact, these weapons were so destructive that they killed large numbers of civilians, not just soldiers. Weapons like these are now called weapons of mass destruction.

Two FDNY paramedics, eager to rescue victims after the World Trade Center attacks, walk the silent streets near the Brooklyn Bridge on September 11, 2001. Many firefighters and policemen rushed to the scene of the attacks in an effort to save as many lives as possible, only to perish in the fire and collapse of the Twin Towers.

Weapons of mass destruction include nuclear weapons, which use atomic energy to create blasts so powerful and emit radiation so poisonous that using them in warfare might wipe out all life on Earth. But there are two less-famous types of weapons of mass destruction that can also have devastating effects on human beings and the environment. Chemical and biological weapons are in many ways more deadly than bullets or bombs, because they are invisible to the human eye. They don't need powerful explosives or huge missiles to be effective. They can be sprayed into the air over armies or towns, killing most of the people who breathe them in or are touched by them. They can linger in the soil, killing new groups of people if they are accidentally stirred up. They can be used to poison water supplies. They can be used to infect inno-cent people who then spread them to others.

Until September 11, 2001, few people in the United States outside of the military thought much about these kinds of weapons. But on that day, members of Al Qaeda, an Islamic terrorist group led by Saudi Arabian Osama bin Laden, hijacked four passenger planes. Two were crashed deliberately into the Twin Towers of the World Trade Center in New York City, killing the passengers, office workers in the towers, and emergency workers who rushed to the scene and were killed when the towers collapsed. A third plane was brought down in a Pennsylvania field, most likely after its passengers decided to attack the hijackers before they could crash into another building. The fourth plane crashed into the Pentagon outside Washington, D.C., raising the toll of the dead even higher.

After such a massive terrorist attack on U.S. citizens, fears of other kinds of attacks began to grow as well. The United States government worries that terrorist groups such as Al Qaeda might decide to use chemical and biological weapons the next time they try to attack. In the following chapters, we will explore the history and effectiveness of these weapons of mass destruction, and how the United States is defending its citizens against them after September 11. ■

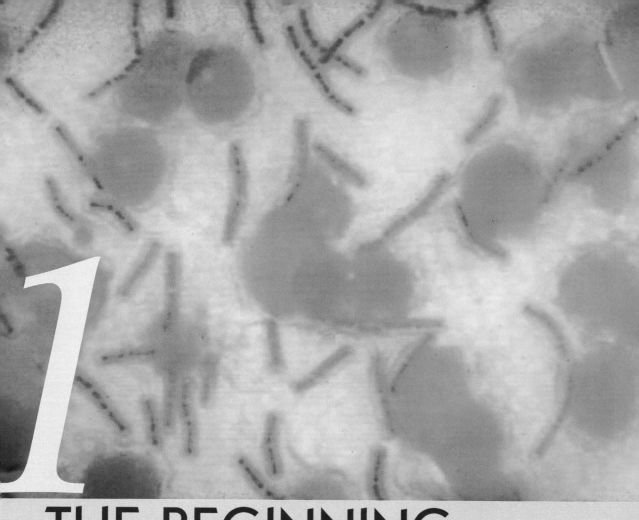

1 THE BEGINNING OF BIOLOGICAL WARFARE

A biological weapon is any living agent, or a toxin made from a once living agent—such as a virus or a bacterium—that is used to attack a country, a group, or an individual. There are many kinds of biological weapons. Most biological weapons are natural viruses or bacteria that have been modified in a lab to be more deadly and easier to use against an enemy. Some biological weapons have been specially created in a lab by combining bits and pieces of different organisms. Since biological weapons first began to be manufactured in the early twentieth century, even more deadly types have been created.

But even before humans began to make their own biological weapons, some people had figured out how to use disease as a weapon of war. Ancient Greek armies dipped arrows in the blood of decomposing bodies, creating poisonous weapons. Roman and Persian soldiers dumped dead animals into wells to contaminate a town's water supply. In the 1340s, Mongol soldiers used the bubonic plague to their advantage by hurling infected bodies over the walls of the Russian city they were attacking.

When Europeans conquered the New World, they caused an accidental form of biological warfare. Europeans brought diseases with them that the Native Americans had never been exposed to before. And while explorers like Juan Ponce de León fought and killed many Native Americans in battle, many more Native Americans died from the new diseases, such as smallpox, that their immune systems had no defense against. Later European forces, such as the British during the French and Indian War (1754–1763), used this knowledge of the Native Americans' weakness. Lord Jeffery Amherst, commanding general of the British, ordered his troops to give the Delaware Indians blankets and handkerchiefs that had been used by smallpox victims during the French and Indian War.

But until germs began to be understood, they could not become major weapons. Until the late nineteenth and early twentieth centuries, no one really understood how disease spread. They knew that touching dead bodies or sick people (or things that had touched them) could sometimes spread sickness, but they did not know why.

This is a microscopic view of the anthrax bacteria, known as *Bacillus anthracis*. The bacteria produce spores that are able to lie dormant in soil for many years, and then enter an animal or person through inhalation, digestion, or contact with skin. It is most commonly found in wild and domestic cattle. Livestock can be regularly vaccinated against anthrax.

This depiction of a smallpox victim attempts to portray the devastation suffered by the Native Americans in the New World. Smallpox is a uniquely human disease. Only humans can carry the disease; it cannot be transferred to or by animals. By the 1500s, the disease had long existed in western Europe. There, large populations in cities provided the conditions for the chain of infection to continue unbroken until a level of immunity could be established.

THE SCIENCE OF DISEASE

For most of early human history, the cause of disease was unknown. When people fell ill, they might believe a god was angry with them, or that an evil spirit possessed them. Over time, it was discovered that some plants, such as willow bark, were good for treating the patient's symptoms. But most often, surviving an illness was a matter of luck for the patient.

Discovering how disease worked took many decades and involved many different scientists. Antoni van Leeuwenhoek (1632–1723), a Dutch naturalist, invented one of the first microscopes, which allowed microorganisms to be seen. Lady Mary Montagu (1689–1762) brought an ancient technique of smallpox vaccination to Europe from Turkey. Later, Edward Jenner (1749–1823) and Louis Pasteur (1822–1895) developed stronger and safer vaccines against smallpox and other diseases. Meanwhile, the knowledge that many germs grew best in dirty and waste-filled environments led to a hygiene movement. Joseph Lister (1827–1912), Ignaz Semmelweis (1818–1865), and other doctors proved that cleaner hospitals prevented patient infections. Sewage treatment and food handling improved, keeping more germs out of food and water.

But many diseases still needed medicines to treat them. More and more laboratories began learning how to culture germs so that they could experiment on them. This resulted in many great gains in medicine, such as the discovery of the first antibiotic, penicillin, in 1928 by Alexander Fleming (1881–1955). Death from disease began to slow down. Smallpox was eradicated outside of the lab by 1977.

Through experimentation, scientists had come to understand a great deal about how various types of microorganisms grow, reproduce, and die. Yet, by the early part of the twentieth century, some scientists and their governments had also started to speculate on another role for germs. They now knew how to keep germs alive and carry them from place to place. It was not a great leap to consider whether these germs could be used to make a new type of weapon.

DISEASE BECOMES A MODERN-DAY WEAPON

As more and more was understood about disease and how it spread, powerful nations began exploring ways to use disease as a weapon. It

11

TYPES OF GERMS

What is a germ? The word "germ" comes from the Latin word *germen*, or "bud." In medical terms, germs are microorganisms that can spread disease. There are four types: bacteria, viruses, rickettsia, and fungi. During the height of the Cold War, the United States and the Soviet Union experimented with nearly all of these germs. Some, like anthrax (a bacterium), proved easier to weaponize than others, like types of fungi.

Bacteria are organisms made up of a single cell. They are the smallest living organisms that can reproduce without a host organism to live in. They are the oldest living form on Earth, and appeared approximately 3.5 billion years ago. Most kinds of bacteria are neutral or even helpful to humans, such as the bacteria that live in our bodies to help us digest food. But bacteria also cause many diseases, including anthrax, brucellosis, bubonic plague, cholera, tularemia, and typhoid fever. They can also create toxins, like botulinum, that cause sickness in humans.

Viruses are simple organisms. They are parasites, which means they cannot reproduce by themselves. They are made up of bits of protein, and must find a host to live in to survive. They attack the host by penetrating its cells and forcing those cells to make more viruses. They can be spread by touch,

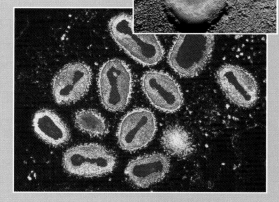

The rodlike parasitic rickettsias (above) usually infect ticks and mites, and then are transferred to mammals. The virus smallpox (below) can be spread by cough droplets or pus from the pustules of an infected person.

sneezing, or bodily fluids. Even though they reproduce, there is a lot of debate among scientists as to whether viruses are living things or not. Diseases caused by viruses include smallpox, Ebola, yellow fever, AIDS, and the common cold.

Rickettsia are bacteria, but unlike many bacteria, they cannot survive without a host to live in. They are named for Howard T. Ricketts, an American scientist who discovered that they were the cause of Rocky Mountain spotted fever and typhus in 1906. Sadly, he died of typhus himself in 1910. Diseases caused by rickettsia also include Q fever and Brill-Zinsser disease.

Fungi come in thousands of varieties. They can be divided into parasitic fungi, which live off of plants or animals, and saprophytes, which feed off (and help decompose) dead plants or animals. For humans, fungi cause mostly harmless infections like tinea (ringworm) or athlete's foot. But in someone who is already ill, an attack by a fungus can cause real damage. Some types of fungi grow in the lungs when their spores are inhaled and can be fatal.

was during World War I (1914–1918) that the first crude attempts at modern biological warfare would begin.

The Germans targeted livestock (horses, cattle, and sheep) in neutral countries that were scheduled to be shipped to the Allies. Using inoculations and contaminated feed, they infected the livestock with glanders (a disease of the lungs and skin) and anthrax. However, this appears to have had little effect on the Allies, and Germany lost the war.

After the war's end, both chemical and biological weapons were banned by the 1925 Geneva Protocol, a resolution banning certain types of weapons and regulating the treatment of prisoners. However, the protocol did not ban research and development of such weapons. Even so, the United States did not ratify it for fifty years, and Japan refused to sign it at all.

WORLD WAR II

The first well-organized and large-scale use of germ warfare occurred in World War II (1939–1945). Both sides, the Axis powers and the Allies, began the first serious experimentation and stockpiling of germ weapons during the war. However, the weapons themselves were not used much, partly because of the crudeness of the technology available. It was still difficult to infect an enemy army without infecting your own. In addition, effective ways of dropping germs on civilian populations had not been fully developed. As we shall see, while Russia may have experimented with biological weapons, only Japan used germ warfare extensively in World War II.

In his book *Biohazard*, Ken Alibek, a former director of Soviet bioweapons research in the 1980s, describes his belief that the Russians may have used germ warfare in the 1942 Battle of Stalingrad. During that battle, many German and Russian troops came down with tularemia, a bacterial disease that causes fever and swelling of the lymph nodes, in numbers that were much higher than usual. While doing research on germ warfare for the Soviet Union, Alibek became intrigued by the tularemia outbreak at Stalingrad and asked his Soviet commander if the outbreak had been caused on purpose. His director refused to confirm it, but Alibek remained convinced that the outbreak was no accident.

The real truth of what happened in Stalingrad may never be known, but Japan's germ warfare attacks on China, beginning in 1936, are much better documented. Japan had an extensive and ruthless germ warfare program during World War II. As many as 10,000 people were killed in germ warfare experiments, most of them prisoners. The notorious Unit 731 of the Japanese army conducted horrific experiments on prisoners, infecting them with diseases such as anthrax, cholera, typhoid, and bubonic plague. Unit 731 was responsible for what has been dubbed the "Asian Holocaust" that was as brutal, though on a smaller scale, as the Germans' treatment of the Jews.

Using what they learned experimenting on prisoners, by 1940 Japan was dropping ceramic containers with bubonic plague–infested fleas on the Chinese countryside, as well as poisoning wells and food supplies. Infected food was given out to Chinese villagers as "gifts" from the Japanese

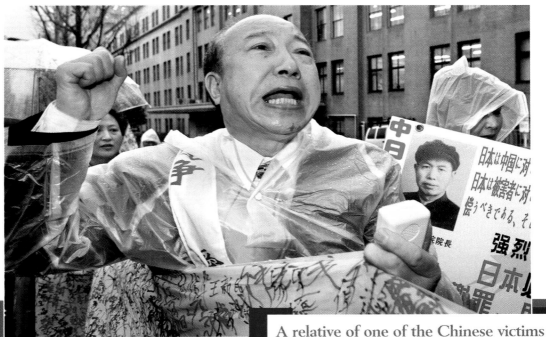

A relative of one of the Chinese victims of Unit 731's germ warfare marched to demand an apology and compensation from the Japanese government on March 18, 2004, in Tokyo, Japan. As many as 180 relatives of the victims are suing the Japanese government. So far, the Japanese government has only acknowledged that Unit 731 existed. No apologies or compensation have been offered.

government. Children were given "inoculations" that were really deadly infections. Hundreds of thousands of people may have died as a result of these attacks.

Yet little has been known about the extent of the atrocities until recently. Many records were destroyed when the Japanese surrendered in 1945. Even now, Japan is reluctant to disclose the full extent of its World War II germ warfare, although new books drawing on the records of Chinese survivors and the confessions of Japanese soldiers continue to increase the public's awareness and may help bring about justice to Japan's victims.

THE COLD WAR

After World War II, tensions between the USSR and the United States continued to rise. Both sides began stockpiling weapons of mass destruction along with conventional weapons. Eventually, enough nuclear weapons to eliminate all life on Earth several times over were stockpiled on both sides. Still, this was not enough. The distrust and hostility between the two countries ran so deep that they continued to develop biological weapons at an incredible rate.

Both nations researched weapons and ways of dispersing them that could cause the most damage to the enemy. Both nations spied on each other's programs, even taking samples of soil or water where they knew the other had done experiments. Finally, in 1969, U.S. president Richard Nixon terminated the U.S. offensive biological weapons program and ordered weapons stocks destroyed. The United States switched to focusing on prevention, detection, and inoculation against germ weapons.

In 1972, the United States, the Soviet Union, and more than 100 nations signed the Biological and Toxin Weapons Convention, which banned all such weapons. But there was no clear way to enforce the treaty. The Soviet Union secretly kept up its deadly weapon experiments.

According to Alibek, the Soviet program was like nothing ever seen before. Whole factories, scattered all across the Soviet Union, were devoted to growing biological agents such as anthrax, plague, and Marburg disease. Nearly any deadly disease known to man was researched to see if it could be made into a weapon. If researchers were careless in these labs, they themselves often suffered a gruesome death. The secrecy of the Soviet weapons programs makes it impossible to know how many died. But when an accident occurred at a town named Sverdlovsk in 1979, it was too horrifying for even the Soviets to cover up.

SVERDLOVSK

Sverdlovsk, now known as Yekaterinburg, is a medium-sized mining community in the Ural Mountains in the Ukraine. In the 1970s, it became the secret home of an anthrax-producing facility run by Biopreparat, the USSR's biological weapons administration. On the morning of April 2, 1979, a missing filter on an air-circulation vent allowed aerosolized anthrax spores into the outside air. People and animals in the path of the spores immediately began falling sick. Sixty-four people died within six weeks. When word of the epidemic leaked out, the Soviets claimed it was caused by tainted meat. Some Western scientists found this plausible, but

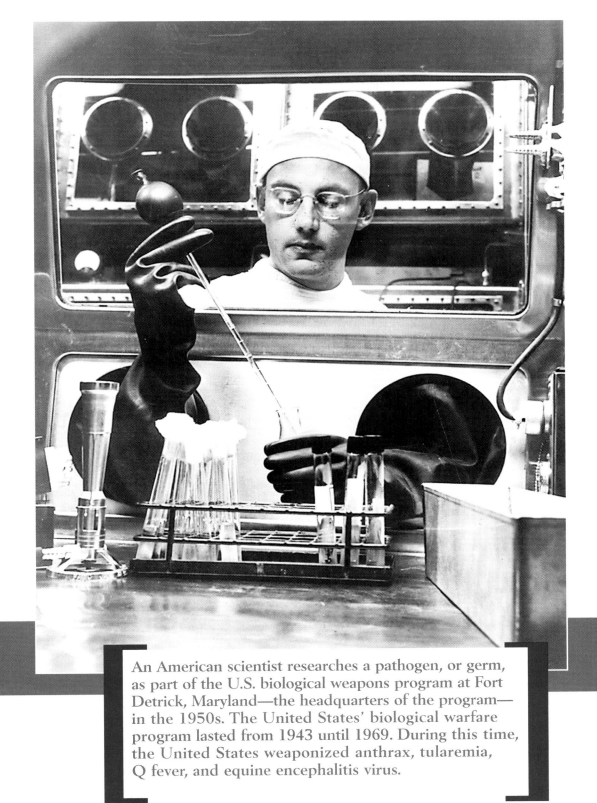

An American scientist researches a pathogen, or germ, as part of the U.S. biological weapons program at Fort Detrick, Maryland—the headquarters of the program—in the 1950s. The United States' biological warfare program lasted from 1943 until 1969. During this time, the United States weaponized anthrax, tularemia, Q fever, and equine encephalitis virus.

A group of Russian researchers try on their protective gear in this undated photo at the Shikhany research center, one of the most important sites for chemical and biological weapons testing in the former Soviet Union. Though the Soviet Union had ratified the Biological and Toxin Weapons Convention (BWC) in 1975, it violated the treaty by continuing to produce a massive biological offensive program. It is believed that some sites in Russia continue to develop a biological weapons program today.

others did not. It was not until 1992 that President Boris Yeltsin admitted that the outbreak was caused by a biological weapons facility. He allowed a team of Western scientists to visit Sverdlovsk and interview the residents and survivors, although not to visit the facility itself. By taking lung samples from the survivors, the scientists were able to tell that the victims had come down with a weaponized form of anthrax, not with naturally occurring anthrax.

After the fall of the Soviet Union, the large bioweapons factories were shut down. But stores of Soviet bioweapons factories, and the knowledge to make more, may still pose a threat if they fall into the wrong hands, as we will explore in the next chapter. ∎

Two hazardous materials workers get sprayed down after leaving the Longworth House Office Building on Capitol Hill in Washington, D.C., in October 2001. Traces of anthrax had been discovered in the offices of three congressmen. Experts believe the source of the 2001 anthrax attacks was a U.S. army biological weapons plant.

BIOTERRORISM

Since the end of the Cold War in 1991, there have been no nations likely to deliberately provoke war with the United States. It remains the sole super-power, and smaller nations would have no hope against it in conventional warfare. But there are terrorist and guerilla groups, such as Al Qaeda, which see the United States as a destructive and evil force, and which will use whatever weapons they can to strike back.

Terrorism is not a new form of warfare. Small groups have always used whatever weapons they could find against a larger enemy. But terrorist groups that use

SEEKING
INFORMATION

ADNAN G. EL SHUKRIJUMAH

Aliases: Adnan G. El Shukri Jumah, Abu Arif, Ja'far Al-Tayar, Jaffar Al-Tayyar, Jafar Tayar, Jaafar Al-Tayyar

DESCRIPTION

Date of Birth Used:	August 4, 1975	Hair:	Black
Place of Birth:	Saudi Arabia	Eyes:	Black
Height:	5'3" to 5'6"	Sex:	Male
Weight:	132 pounds	Complexion:	Dark, Mediterranean
Build:	Average		

Remarks: El Shukrijumah occasionally wears a beard. He has a pronounced nose and is asthmatic. El Shukrijumah speaks English and carries a Guyanese passport, but may attempt to enter the United States with a Saudi, Canadian, or Trinidadian passport.

DETAILS

Adnan G. El Shukrijumah is wanted in connection with possible terrorist threats against the United States.

REWARD

The Rewards For Justice Program, United States Department of State, is offering a reward of up to $5 million dollars for information leading directly to the capture of Adnan G. El Shukrijumah.

SHOULD BE CONSIDERED ARMED AND DANGEROUS

CONTACT INFORMATION

IF YOU HAVE ANY INFORMATION CONCERNING THIS PERSON, PLEASE CONTACT THE LOCAL FBI OFFICE OR THE NEAREST

"cells" inside the country of their enemy have become a new concern for the United States since September 11. These cells might make use of biological and chemical weapons to create havoc and disrupt society.

The current government of Russia claims that it no longer produces or stores biological weapons. However, there is still concern that such weapons may have found their way to individuals or groups outside the government after the Soviet Union's collapse. There is the possibility, experts believe, that former Bio-preparat scientists may have put their knowledge for sale in the under-ground weapons markets. Although most biological weapons have a short shelf life, there is no guarantee that the knowledge to make them will not find its way into the hands of govern-ments looking for new weapons against the United States and its allies.

FBI director Robert Mueller points out four photos depicting various disguises of a suspected terrorist at a news conference held on May 26, 2004. It is believed that Al Qaeda has planned more attacks against the United States. At this conference, it was not known what form the attack would take that they were warning against, yet these photos were shown to alert law enforcement officers as well as the general public.

Disciples gather at the feet of Bhagwan Shree Rajneesh in this undated photo in Rajneeshpuram, Oregon. When the cult members spiked ten salad bars with salmonella, it was the first attack of germ warfare within the United States. Victims of salmonella poisoning experience diarrhea, fever, and abdominal cramps that usually last four to seven days. Although most people can recover without treatment, the bacteria can enter the bloodstream and spread if not treated properly.

Shortly before the end of the Cold War and since its end, the main threat of bioterrorism has come from small terrorist or cult groups. Many of these have used biological weapons not to cause mass destruction, but to create terror and to gain attention for their religious or political messages.

THE SHREE RAJNEESH BIOATTACKS

In a small rural area of Oregon in the fall of 1984, tensions were running high between local citizens and the members of a nearby religious commune, headed by the Indian guru Bhagwan Shree Rajneesh. The commune wished to get its own members elected to the county's government and take it over. Before and during election day, commune members poisoned ten salad bars in the area with salmonella, causing more than 750 people to subsequently become sick. At first, authorities thought it was the fault of the restaurants, but they later learned the truth while investigating the commune's other illegal activities. In 1985, Rajneesh himself was convicted of visa fraud and deported to India, where he later died. Several of his followers also went to prison. This was the first bioterrorist act on American soil, but it attracted little attention at the time.

Although most infamous for a chemical-weapons attack, which will be covered in chapter 4, the Aum Shinrikyo cult also made many attempts at biological warfare. Between 1993 and 1995, this Japanese cult tried as many as ten times to spray botulinum toxin and anthrax in downtown Tokyo. The attacks were unsuccessful, possibly because the agents were not weapon-grade.

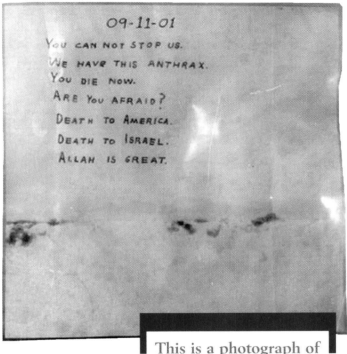

This is a photograph of the letter that accompanied the anthrax sent to Senate Majority Leader Tom Daschle in October 2001. The letter was opened by a staff member, who was then immediately treated for anthrax poisoning. There was no clear evidence as to why Daschle was chosen to receive the letter.

THE 2001 ANTHRAX ATTACKS

Just a week after the terrible events of September 11, 2001, a letter containing

SELECTED BIOLOGICAL AGENTS AND THEIR EFFECTS

Agent	Disease	Effects
Bacterium	Anthrax	Incubation period of one to six days. After incubation, respiratory distress or skin blisters develop. Shock and death can follow within twenty-four to thirty-six hours.
Bacterium	Bubonic plague	Incubation period of two to three days. After incubation, fever, coma, and respiratory failure can occur, leading to death within forty-eight hours.
Virus	Smallpox	Incubation varies. After incubation, high fever for one to two days, followed by rashes on the trunk or limbs and then skin eruptions ("pox"). Often fatal if untreated.
Virus	Venezuelan equine encephalitis (VEE)	Incubation period of one to five days. After incubation, fever, headache, and extreme sensitivity to light often occur for twenty-four to seventy-two hours. Lethargy may follow for one to two weeks. Can be fatal.
Virus	Yellow fever	Incubation period of several days. After incubation, headache, backache, fever, nausea, and vomiting appear for two to three days. Patient then begins to recover or proceeds to high fever, slow pulse rate, vomiting blood, and death.
Rickettsia	Q fever	Incubation period of ten to twenty days. After incubation, fever, cough, and chest pain may last up to two weeks. Can be fatal.

Agent	Disease	Effects
Toxin	Botulinum exposure	Symptoms can be immediate or delayed. They include dry mouth; difficulty seeing, speaking, or swallowing; nausea; vomiting; and dizziness. Can progress to paralysis and respiratory failure, leading to death.
Toxin	Ricin poisoning	Symptoms within two to twenty-four hours. They include abdominal pain, vomiting and diarrhea (often with blood), dehydration, fever, and shock. Death can occur within thirty-six to forty-eight hours.

anthrax spores was mailed to Tom Brokaw at NBC News in New York. Two other letters with nearly identical handwriting, threatening messages, and lethal spores arrived at the offices of the *New York Post* and Senator Tom Daschle in Washington, D.C.

By the end of the year, eighteen people had been infected with anthrax and five people had died. Many mysteries remain in the case. A woman in Connecticut and a woman in New York City both contracted anthrax and died in 2001, but authorities were not able to find out how they had been infected. No spores or letters were found near their homes or workplaces. Two employees of a company named American Media, Inc., also contracted anthrax, and spores were found in their building, though no letter could be found. In fact, Bob Stevens at American Media was the first victim of the attacks to die. It is still not known who sent the letters, although a domestic terrorist, not Al Qaeda or any other foreign group, is currently suspected. In August 2004, a bioterrorism expert who is also a founder of an organization

The bride and groom kiss through their face masks while posing for their wedding photographs in Beijing, China, in May 2003. SARS was clearly not a bioweapon, yet it was an epidemic that called for such precautions as this. China has been the site of two-thirds of the world's SARS cases. By late April 2004, no new SARS cases had been reported.

that trains medical professionals in how to respond to chemical and biological attacks was being investigated by the Federal Bureau of Investigation, or FBI. Authorities have conducted 5,200 interviews in connection with the 2001 anthrax attacks. In the meantime, many postal sorting offices now use low-level radiation to kill any potential biological agents in the mail.

THE FUTURE OF BIOLOGICAL WEAPONS

Continuing to create biological weapons is a risky business for any country to engage in. We are still limited in our understanding of how disease works, and the danger is even greater now that we are learning to manipulate the DNA of various life-forms, such as when genetically modified mice are used in experiments. It is possible that we will create a disease for which there is no available cure. Should such a disease get out of the lab and into the human population, there is no telling how much death and suffering would result. For example, if a strain of influenza that resisted antibiotics was released, we might see a repeat of the 1918 influenza epidemic, which killed 20 to 40 million people. In a time in our history when human beings travel to every point of the globe, there is no way to ensure that such a disease can be contained. Our experience with yearly flu viruses and the recent SARS epidemic has taught us that. As we will see in chapter 5, guarding against such a tragedy requires a great deal of planning and precaution. ■

3 THE BEGINNING OF CHEMICAL WARFARE

At 5:00 PM on April 22, 1915, German troops at Ypres, Belgium, were given a historic order. They were to discharge 198 tons (180,000 kilograms) of chlorine gas downwind toward the Allied troops. Pushed by the favoring breeze, the deadly cloud billowed toward the French and Algerians stationed there. As the gas reached them, the troops began to flee or fall, opening a gap in the Allied line.

Blinded French soldiers are led by their comrades after the Battle of the Marne in July 1918. The Marne is a river northeast of Paris, France. The battle began with an attack by the Germans, but ended in an Allied victory. The Germans are thought to have used about 68,000 (61.7 million Kg)tons of gas during World War I. The French utilized 36,000 tons and the British used 25,000 tons.

This was the first major chemical weapons offensive.

It's no wonder the soldiers fled. Exposure to chlorine gas causes burns to the skin, blindness, vomiting, and internal bleeding. Its symptoms can be apparent right away or show up hours later. All in all, 125,000 tons (113.4 million kg) of chemical weapons were used during World War I, by both the Allies and the Germans. As at Ypres, they were often dispersed in gas form, but that was dangerous for the deploying side if the wind shifted. The British, French,

U.S. soldiers are pictured here in various styles of gas masks worn during World War I. World War I was set off when European powers quickly drew up sides when tensions culminated into the assassination of Franz Ferdinand, the heir to the Austro-Hungarian Empire. The United States entered the war in 1917, at the request of the Allied powers: France, Great Britain, and Russia, against Germany, Austria-Hungary, and Turkey.

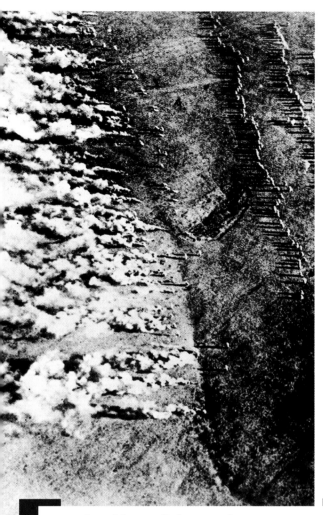

and Germans all developed mortars (large missiles) that could be filled with liquid chemical agents and fired at the enemy.

Modern chemical weapons did not often cause immediate death, nor were they meant to. Those who used them understood that a wounded soldier, needing care, slowed an enemy army more than a dead soldier.

THE HISTORY OF CHEMICAL WEAPONS

Chemical weaponry had been used in a limited way since ancient times. Most of these weapons were in the form of incendiary devices— weapons that when hurled would start a fire. These included pots filled with chemicals that would burst into flames when they shattered against an enemy ship or fortress. Indian and Chinese armies also knew some secrets of chemical warfare. One army generated poison gases to fill a tunnel, smothering enemy troops who were digging under fortress walls.

But a science of chemistry did not really develop until the eighteenth and nineteenth centuries. Russian chemist Dmitry Mendeleyev's creation of the

French soldiers *(left)* guard against a German warfare attack in 1915. By using chemicals, armies saw a way out of the stalemate that trench warfare had caused. The French were the first to use chemicals as weapons when they launched a tear gas attack in 1914. However, the Germans were the first to use it on a massive scale, as pictured in the above photo of an attack during World War I.

periodic table in 1869 helped scientists understand the properties of the different elements that make up chemicals. Other discoveries about the nature of molecules and atoms, along with improvements in laboratory equipment, created great advances in the science of chemistry. Part of the success of the Industrial Revolution was a result of new chemical technologies for creating dyes, solvents, and lubricants.

But with the ability to create powerful chemicals in large quantities came the knowledge that many of these chemicals were harmful to humans. Workers in the new factories that used toxic chemicals began to complain of bad health and side effects. The terrible smoke, smog,

THE FIRST CHEMICAL WEAPONRY

The major chemical weapons used by both sides in World War I include:

■ Chlorine: A common chemical used in water purification that burns and destroys lung tissue.

■ Hydrogen cyanide: An extremely poisonous chemical gas that can smell like almonds. It was later used to execute prisoners in Nazi Germany and was also used at one time in the United States. It shuts down cell respiration, leading to death.

■ Chloropicrin: A pesticide that is also dangerous to humans. Causes irritation of the skin and eyes, and may have a sweet smell. Usually not fatal, but could cause permanent eye damage.

■ Mustard gas: Not actually a gas, but instead a light yellow, oily liquid which becomes a gas above a certain temperature. It blisters the skin and also burns the lungs. It sometimes smells like garlic or mustard.

and waste caused by some factories made air and water pollution a problem for those who lived nearby.

By the time World War I began, some military strategists and scientists decided to take advantage of these toxic side effects. With their new technologies, they believed they could make toxic chemicals a major weapon in their arsenal. After the attack at Ypres, chemical warfare research exploded, until nearly every combatant was using some form of gas or liquid against their enemies. It proved surprisingly easy to make new chemical weapons. This is because almost any highly concentrated chemical can be harmful in the right amounts.

Despite the amount of suffering, death, and long-term damage to survivors caused by chemical warfare in World War I, most historians agree it did not determine the outcome of the war. As a battlefield weapon, chemicals were not terribly effective. Spraying liquids or gases on an enemy is always risky for an army, because wind shifts can bring the chemicals back toward the attackers. On the other hand, a lack of wind may mean that deadly chemicals linger, making the ground that the attackers gain in battle dangerous to them as well. Chemicals that stay in soil or in water supplies are just as dangerous to the invaders who used them as to those who were attacked.

In addition, the soldiers who have to handle dangerous chemicals run a high risk of being poisoned themselves; not to mention the civilian workers who create the chemical weapons. The more deadly the weapon, the more likely that those who use it will suffer casualties, too. Chemical weapons also tend to be extremely unstable, with a short shelf life. This means that an army that wants to use chemical weapons has to be able to create great quantities of them quickly, which is expensive and dangerous.

After World War I, the League of Nations declared that there was no justification for using chemical weapons in war. The Treaty of Versailles in 1919 forbade the manufacture of chemical weapons in Germany. Later, in 1925, the Protocol for the Prohibition of the Use in War of Asphyxiating, Poisonous, or Other Gases, and of Bacteriological Methods of Warfare was signed and ratified in Geneva, Switzerland. But the League of Nations

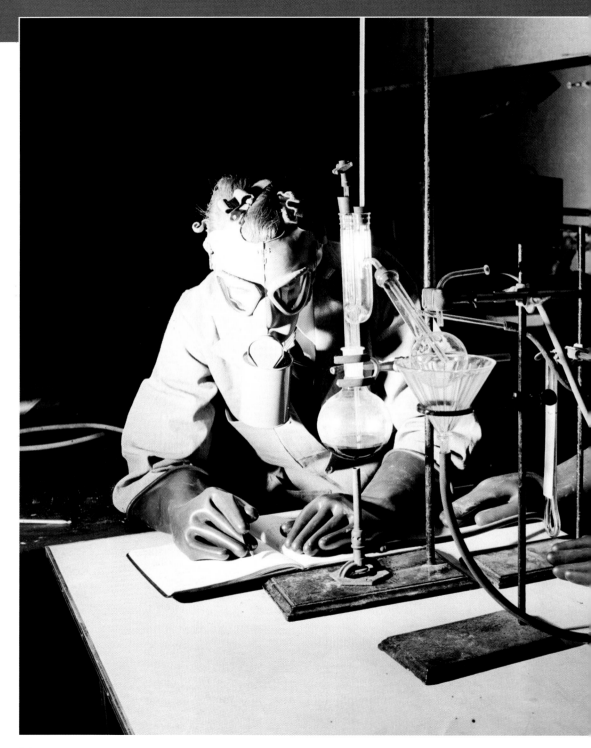

These scientists *(left)* are in the process of preparing a batch of mustard gas in 1942. Mustard gas was used in large amounts during World Wars I and II, probably because it can be easily dispersed via bombs, artillery shells, and rockets. Also, an area contaminated with mustard gas is unusable by enemy forces. Above: These Londoners were prepared for a possible gas attack by the Germans during World War II.

could not enforce the protocol, and it remained up to the signers of the protocol to follow it and to make sure that other nations followed it. In fact, the United States did not officially sign the protocol until 1975, and may have kept stores of chemical weapons until the late 1950s.

Most likely, it was the ineffectiveness of chemical weapons and not the Geneva Protocol that explains why chemicals have rarely been used since World War I. Although there is evidence that many signers of the protocol still had chemical weapons in World War II and may have used them in some battles, they did not play a major role in warfare. In fact, while the government of Great Britain handed out gas masks to a great number of its citizens in case of a German gas attack, none occurred. Some speculate that this was because Adolf Hitler had

Here, Agent Orange is being sprayed over an area of South Vietnam in 1966. The purpose of spraying this defoliant chemical was to expose Vietcong forces as they moved through the dense forest. Unfortunately, the effects of Agent Orange were underestimated. It has since been linked to cancer in Vietnamese who were exposed to it, as well as the U.S. soldiers who sprayed it. Agent Orange has also been linked to birth defects in the children of those exposed to it.

suffered from gas poisoning himself as a soldier in World War I, and so was reluctant to use it as a weapon.

Chemical agents were still used in another way after World War I. Nonlethal agents like tear gas became a tool for riot control by police and the military. Defoliants (chemicals that kill plant life) like Agent Orange were used in the Vietnam War (1955–1975) to burn the dense forests that hid the United States' Communist opponents. Although Agent Orange was not supposed to be harmful to people, many Vietnam veterans believe exposure to it led to later health problems.

There is evidence that the United States and other governments also experimented with nerve agents (chemicals that interfere with the nervous system) and psychoagents (chemicals that cause hallucinations and mental confusion). But these were also considered ineffective and were never used in battle. ■

4
MODERN
CHEMICAL
WARFARE
After World War I, chemical weapons may have fallen out of favor as a major battlefield weapon, but they remained a powerful tool for creating terror and disruption. Because they are also fairly cheap to produce on a small scale, they are attractive to groups or governments that cannot afford to make nuclear weapons.

Civilians and livestock died during the three-day attack that consisted of mustard gas, sarin, tabun, VX gas, and possibly cyanide. In 1988, Halabja had a population of 70,000 and is located near the Iranian border. Besides the 5,000 who immediately perished, 7,000 were injured or suffered long-term illness. Traces of the chemical agents are reported to still reside in the air, food, and water.

SADDAM HUSSEIN AND THE KURDS

One of the most notorious uses of chemical weapons occurred in 1988. On March 16, Saddam Hussein, the dictator of Iraq, launched an attack on the Kurds in northern Iraq, a group that had long fought for their independence from Saddam. Terrified villagers in Halabja and the surrounding area had become used to hearing bombs fall and explode nearby while the Iran-Iraq War (1980–1990) raged around them. But this time it was different. Bombs fell, but there was no explosion. Within a few minutes, animals began to die. Leaves fell from the trees. As the telltale smells of apples, garlic, and sulfur drifted through the air, many of the Kurds began to get sick, and throughout the next few days, they began to die.

These are the graves of most of the victims of the March 16, 1988, chemical attacks ordered by Saddam Hussein against the Kurds who revolted against his regime during the Iran-Iraq War at the time. This site is located in Halabja, Iraq. At least 5,000 civilians, mainly women and children, immediately perished in the chemical attacks.

Researchers later determined that Saddam most likely used mustard gas, powerful nerve agents like VX (an extremely deadly, odorless liquid) and sarin (an equally lethal gas or liquid), and perhaps defoliants on the Kurd villages. The number of victims is unknown, but it is believed that up to 10 percent of the Kurdish population—4 million people—may have been exposed to chemical, and possibly biological, weapons during the attacks. Ironically, Saddam had obtained at least some of his chemical weapons and equipment from the United States, which had armed him in the 1980s because it saw him as an ally against Iran. There is evidence that Saddam used these chemical weapons against Iran during the Iran-Iraq War of the early 1980s.

The attack against the Kurds was not an attempt to wipe them out completely, but to terrorize them into submission. However, it remains the only known instance of a government using chemical weapons against its own citizens. In the aftermath, more than eleven years later, doctors report that birth defects, cancers, and other health problems are still higher than normal among the Iraqi Kurds.

AUM SHINRIKYO

On June 27, 1994, a secretive Japanese cult began its war against the government of Japan. Members of the group drove to the quiet Tokyo suburb of Matsumoto and released a cloud of the deadly nerve agent sarin. Within days, seven people were dead and many others sick and injured. It was later learned that the cult Aum Shinrikyo had planned the attack as revenge against some judges who lived in the area. These judges sat on a panel that was about to hear a real-estate dispute in which the Japanese cult was a defendant. The cult's leader, Shoko Asahara, believed that he was the leader of a new, pure race and that anyone who stood in his way deserved death. Many of his followers were bright college students with scientific knowledge that allowed them to manufacture chemical and biological weapons.

The attack on Matsumoto emboldened Asahara, and he decided to launch his biggest attack yet: this time, on the Tokyo subway system,

THE TYPES AND EFFECTIVENESS OF CHEMICAL WEAPONS

Chemical weapons can be classified into two main categories: persistent and nonpersistent agents. Persistent agents are dangerous for a considerable period of time after delivery. This means that they tend to stick to surfaces or stay in the air. Nonpersistent agents disperse rapidly after release. These agents are usually meant to be quickly inhaled.

There are many factors that can influence the effectiveness of a chemical agent. These include:

Wind: How an agent disperses depends on wind direction and speed. This is one of the most difficult variables to consider when using chemical weapons.

Temperature: High temperatures tend to break down many agents, while cold temperatures can allow some agents to last longer.

Rain: Rain can dilute some chemical agents. Others may react chemically to water and change to a less-lethal form.

Atmospheric stability: When the air temperature is higher than that of the ground, chemical agents in a vapor state tend to stay persistent for longer periods of time. However when the air temperature is lower than that of the ground, chemical agents in the vapor state tend to disperse more quickly.

The Middle Eastern country of Jordan discovered these chemicals that had been in Al Qaeda's possession. The terrorist group had targeted Jordan's intelligence headquarters in its capital, Amman, for an explosion, using the contents of these jars.

41

Rescue workers and officers help victims of the Aum Shinrikyo sarin attacks on the Tokyo subway on March 20, 1995. The infected subway lines were near government offices in Tokyo. The cult had obtained hundreds of tons of chemicals with the aim of making enough sarin to kill a million people. Sarin was developed by Nazi scientists in Germany in the 1930s. It is said to be 500 times more toxic than cyanide.

especially those parts nearest Tokyo's government buildings. Five men entered five separate subway trains at 8:00 AM on March 20, 1995, with packages containing sarin. Almost simultaneously, they punctured the packages with their umbrellas and left at the next stop, while the deadly fumes began attacking the passengers. The subways were shut down as panic and illness spread. Ambulances streamed in, taking the dead and wounded away, while the whole city came to a standstill. By the time it was over, twelve commuters were dead and 5,500 others were injured. In response, the Japanese government finally decided to shut Aum Shinrikyo down. After several months, Asahara and many of his followers were captured, and his stocks of weapons and money were confiscated. Eventually, Asahara and ten other cult members were sentenced to death, but none has yet been executed.

While Aum Shinrikyo has been stopped, the Tokyo attacks demonstrate how a small fanatical group can use chemical weapons to cause disruption, death, and panic. Since September 11, 2001, the United States and other nations have studied the Tokyo attacks to determine the best ways to deal with weapons that might be used on major U.S. subway systems, such as that in New York City. Chemical weapons, for all their weaknesses, remain a real danger, especially as the technology for delivering them becomes more sophisticated. While they may never become feasible as battlefield weapons, they are very effective at disrupting societies and terrorizing enemies. As we will see in chapter 5, it is their usefulness to terrorist groups that makes monitoring them of great importance to the United States and other nations targeted by terrorists. ■

In this simulation of a toxic gas attack, the toxicity level is being measured with an electronic sniffer. Although civilians are ultimately concerned with how the national government would respond in a chemical or biological warfare attack, the first responders to such an attack would be local personnel and government. That is why it is important that local officials get the proper training and equipment, too.

5

CHEMICAL AND BIOLOGICAL WEAPONS AFTER 9/11

The mysterious anthrax attacks that occurred soon after September 11 only underlined the nation's vulnerability. Postal services and government functions were disrupted while the sources were investigated. Testing and treating everyone who might have been

The 9/11 Commission views a video of the attack on the World Trade Center. The commission released its report in July 2004 after a twenty-month investigation into the terrorist attacks. The bipartisan, independent commission concluded that the nation could have been better prepared and paid closer attention to the warnings that preceded the attacks.

exposed was costly and time consuming, as was decontaminating the buildings the anthrax spores were found in and installing devices to irradiate the mail and kill possible biological agents.

INTELLIGENCE

Since September 11, several weaknesses in the United States' intelligence gathering have been discovered. The 9/11 Commission was an independent, bipartisan commission created by the U.S. Congress to investigate the circumstances that led to the terrorist attacks and how they could have been prevented. The commission found that warning signs were present, but they had not been evaluated in terms of a big picture. According to MSNBC.com's report on the commission's findings, by August 6, 2001, President George W. Bush

> . . . had seen a stream of alarming reports on Al Qaeda's intentions. So had Vice President Cheney and Bush's top national security team . . . In April and May 2001, for example,

the intelligence community headlined some of those reports, "Bin Laden planning multiple operations," "Bin Laden network's plans advancing" and "Bin Laden threats are real." The intelligence included reports of a hostage plot against Americans. It noted that operatives might choose to hijack an aircraft or storm a U.S. embassy. . .

As director of Central Intelligence George Tenet (who has since resigned) told the commission, "The system was blinking red." But not enough people were paying attention. The FBI and Central Intelligence Agency, or CIA, often did not discuss their findings with each other, although both had been tracking what later proved to be Al Qaeda activities. There were not nearly enough Arab and Farsi (the language of modern Iran) translators to go through the intelligence that was gathered. In addition, many of the hijackers were in the United States on expired or false visas. In response, the Immigration and Naturalization Service, or INS, has cracked down on visa fraud, and incoming foreigners to the United States are now subject to much more intense scrutiny. Discussions on how to fix these issues are still ongoing.

> "The system was blinking red."
>
> *George Tenet*

ACCESS

During the investigation into the anthrax mailings of 2001, it was discovered that almost anyone could obtain dangerous bioagents, such as anthrax or smallpox, from various research institutions by posing as scientists. With false documentation, it was easy to get samples of lethal agents and perhaps turn them into weapons. For example, in 1996, an Ohio State student affiliated with a white supremacist group used a fake letterhead to obtain the bacterium that causes the bubonic plague. While the Antiterrorism and Effective Death Penalty Act of 1996 was enacted to prevent this from occurring again, it is not known which germs may have been sent out in the meantime. Researchers at some university labs believe that even after the law was enacted, sloppy procedures may

AL QAEDA AND OSAMA BIN LADEN

Al Qaeda is one of the world's most infamous terrorist organizations. Al Qaeda—which means "the base" in Arabic—is the network of extremists organized by Osama bin Laden. Its origins are in the 1980s uprising against the Soviet occupation of Afghanistan. In the mid-1980s, Osama bin Laden, a wealthy Saudi Arabian, began financing the Afghan resistance and helping recruit new fighters. These warriors, who numbered in the thousands, were crucial in defeating Soviet forces.

Bin Laden had studied with radical Islamic thinkers and was unhappy with the pro-Western policies of the Saudi Arabian government. He was outraged when the Saudis allowed U.S. troops to be stationed in his country, the birthplace of Islam. In 1991, he was expelled from Saudi Arabia for antigovernment activities.

After his expulsion, bin Laden established headquarters for his new organization, Al Qaeda, in Khartoum, Sudan. Al Qaeda's first acts against the United States were attacks on U.S. servicemen in Somalia. In August 1996, bin Laden issued a declaration of war against the United States. In 1996, Sudan—under pressure from Saudi Arabia and the United States—expelled bin Laden, who moved his base of operations to Afghanistan.

Al Qaeda's leadership oversees a loosely organized network

Several videotapes of Osama bin Laden have been released by Al Qaeda. Concern about their propaganda purposes and possible hidden messages to terrorist cells worldwide cause governments to warn media organizations such as CNN about airing them.

of cells. Its infrastructure is small, mobile, and decentralized. Al Qaeda does not depend on the sponsorship of a political state, and it is not defined by a particular war or struggle. Instead, it provides financial and logistical support to terrorist groups operating in the Philippines, Algeria, Eritrea, Afghanistan, Chechnya, Tajikistan, Somalia, Yemen, and Kashmir, among others.

The aims of Al Qaeda are to drive Americans and American influence out of all Muslim nations, especially Saudi Arabia; to destroy Israel; and to topple pro-Western governments around the Middle East. Bin Laden has also said that he wishes to unite all Muslims and establish, by force if necessary, an Islamic nation.

In response to the September 11, 2001, attacks on the United States, the United States invaded Afghanistan in October 2001 to dismantle Al Qaeda and the Taliban, the country's governing regime. Al Qaeda's infrastructure in the country was destroyed and its military commander was killed. Another top operative was captured in Pakistan. Bin Laden, however, escaped and is presumed alive. He still releases audio and video messages to the Arab media from time to time. There have been about a dozen major attacks by Al Qaeda terrorists since September 11, 2001. Osama bin Laden, although in hiding, still plays an important role in shaping the group's mission.

have caused security breaches—by letting too many people have access to the germ cultures in school labs, for example.

After September 11, the United States began inspecting research facilities that might provide access to dangerous germs. Many universities and research institutions also began reviewing their security procedures and even destroying any stocks they had of dangerous bioagents.

Preventing access to chemicals that can be weaponized is much more problematic. Many of them, such as chlorine, have legitimate and legal uses. Instead, the Department of Homeland Security has focused on monitoring technologies for disseminating agents, such as sprayers and crop dusters. Security around such vulnerable sites as water treatment plants has also begun to improve, though many groups complain that it is not enough. One area of concern has been shipping containers that come into the United States, many of which are never inspected. Some intelligence officials, such as those in the Subcommittee on Coast Guard and Maritime Transportation, have expressed concern over this lack of security.

Each year, more than 7,500 commercial vessels make approximately 51,000 port calls, and more than 6 million loaded marine containers enter U.S. ports. Current growth predictions indicate that container cargo will quadruple in the next twenty years. Standard sizes of cargo containers allow cargo to be quickly transferred from ships to trucks or railcars and transported immediately to anywhere in the country. This rapid transfer of cargo is a possible conduit and target for terrorist activities.

However, inspecting these millions of containers remains an enormous task. The committee is currently focused on better record keeping to track container origins and cargo, as well as scanning or X-ray devices to check for explosives or enemy agents.

DETECTION

Although specifics of their methods are classified, the Department of Defense and its Defense Threat Reduction Agency have a number of tools for detecting biological and chemical agents. Some of these are simple, such as tracking a sudden increase in illness or animal deaths that might be caused by a biological or chemical agent. Some are more advanced, such as installing sophisticated "sniffers" at possible targets that can detect agents released in the air and set off an alarm.

PROTECTION

Members of the military who might be exposed to biological o r chemical weapons are given a number of protections. They may be inoculated against anthrax and smallpox. They are given protective suits and taught how to put them on and seal them at a moment's notice.

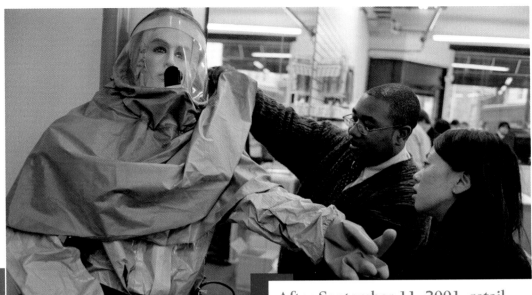

After September 11, 2001, retail stores began to emerge with goods tailored for the new fears and threats brought on by the terrorist attacks. Now it is possible to buy safety kits that include gas masks, duct tape, flashlights, and other equipment. These two customers are inspecting a radiation protection suit at Safer America in New York City.

Civilians are harder to protect. The Department of Homeland Security has many plans in place to make hospitals and communities ready to handle such an attack, and has recommended steps such as inoculating hospital workers against anthrax and other diseases. It has also informed the public of what to do in case of a biological or chemical attack, although it may not always be possible to be absolutely safe. While many private companies do sell biohazard suits and masks, it seems the best protection for civilians is most likely being observant, and reporting any suspicious smells or bags left unattended in high-traffic areas, such as public transportation locations. On July 21, 2004, President Bush signed a bill that would promote stockpiling vaccines and other antidotes (remedies that counteract the effects of poisons) to chemical and biological weapons. The bill gave the drug industry incentives to develop such vaccines, sped up the approval process for them, and allowed the government to use antidotes not yet approved

The terrorists who carried out the 9/11 attacks had visited a small Florida airport and inquired about the capabilities of crop dusters *(above)*. Though numerous precautionary measures concerning crop dusters have been put into place, they are not effective tools for carrying out a biological or chemical attack. Indeed another security alert is subway stations, such as Washington, D.C.'s Metro Rail *(inset)*. Commuters are reminded to stay alert and aware of any suspicious packages or activities.

by the Food and Drug Administration, or FDA, in an emergency if necessary.

SPECULATIONS AND THEORIES ABOUT TERRORIST ATTACKS

Even before September 11, novelists and military strategists have warned about possible terrorist attacks against the United States. These scenarios have become more important as the United States has taken more interest in anticipating terrorist attacks.

- **Subways:** As with the Tokyo terrorist attacks, subways are seen as a natural target. Victims are trapped underground, allowing for easy circulation of a germ or chemical agent. Security around subways has greatly increased since 9/11.

- **Water treatment plants:** Many communities across the United States have started looking at security around water treatment facilities, concerned that a poison or disease-causing agent could be put into the water supply. This is considered a less likely scenario, as it would be difficult for terrorists to put the amount of poison needed into such a large amount of water.

- **Crop dusters:** There is some evidence that Al Qaeda has looked into buying crop-dusting planes, presumably to spread biological or chemical agents over a wide area. However, as with poisoning water supplies, the amount of chemical or biological agents needed to cause widespread destruction is difficult for any group to obtain or create.

- **Nuclear fears:** Security around nuclear plants has increased due to fears that terrorists could fly a plane into them, causing a massive leak of radiation in the surrounding area. "Suitcase bombs" (small nuclear devices) and "dirty bombs" (regular bombs that explode and shower nuclear waste) are also considered potential dangers. With the collapse of the Soviet Union, these fears have increased because of speculation that old Soviet nuclear materials and installations are not being adequately guarded, and might make their way to the black market.

This U.S. marine wears his NBC (nuclear, biological, and chemical) suit after being put on alert of a possible gas attack in Nasiriyah, Iraq, at the beginning of the Iraq War in March 2003. A major reason the United States gave for going to war in the region was the belief of a prolific, unaccounted-for WMD program by the regime of Saddam Hussein. As this information has since been proven to not be accurate, it has deeply divided the American people over the issue of U.S. involvement in the region.

THE SECOND GULF WAR

In 2003, asserting that Saddam Hussein still had the weapons of mass destruction that he used against the Kurds, and that he had ties to Al Qaeda, the United States invaded Iraq. After several months, Saddam himself was captured, but no weapons have yet been found. Many believe that his chemical and biological stockpiles have long since been destroyed by American bombing during the first Gulf War and after. At the time of this book's publication, the situation in Iraq was still far from stable. Combined with the United States' occupation of Afghanistan, this means that the hard task of bringing stability to the Middle East and perhaps reducing terrorism is going to be a long process. The future remains uncertain.

But regardless of how the second Gulf War falls out, it is important to realize that war is not just about weapons. The people who become terrorists or guerillas often do so because they come from places of extreme poverty or oppression, places where they have few opportunities. This does not excuse their actions, but it does give us hope for how we can make such attacks less likely. If we can encourage increased opportunities and political stability in the countries that produce terrorists, it might help to eliminate terrorism altogether. We might be able to make it harder for people such as Osama bin Laden to recruit for their causes. We might start making a world where weapons of mass destruction are both fewer in number and less likely to be used. ■

[GLOSSARY]

anthrax An infectious disease caused by the bacteria *Bacillus anthracis*. It is highly lethal and occurs naturally in many livestock animals such as cattle. Humans can contract anthrax from animals, infected meat, or weaponized spores.

bubonic plague An illness caused by the bacteria *Yersinia pestis* that may have wiped out nearly a third of Europe's population in an epidemic in the fourteenth century. It is called "bubonic" because of the buboes, or swellings, that often form on the victim's skin.

casualties Military personnel who are taken out of battle through death, disease, wounds, or accidents.

Cold War Conflict between the United States and the USSR that took place between the end of World War II and the early 1990s, and that never resulted in direct military action against one another.

cult A group of people with a shared set of religious or philosophical beliefs, often existing on the fringes of society or in secrecy.

defoliant A chemical agent that kills plant life.

DNA Deoxyribonucleic acid. These are the nucleic acids found in cells that are the basic building blocks of life. Manipulating cell DNA can create new forms of life, including more dangerous germs.

fanatic Someone who is completely devoted to a cause or an idea.

intelligence In military terms, any information about a country's enemies that allows it to create a more effective strategy.

regime The person or group of people in charge of a nation.

smallpox A disease caused by the virus of the genus Orthopoxvirus that causes pustules on the skin, and if untreated, often death. As a result of inoculation, it is now believed to exist only in the laboratory.

VX A very powerful nerve agent that blocks the enzyme in the body that prevents muscles from twitching uncontrollably. This disrupts the human nervous system, causing rapid death.

[FOR MORE INFORMATION]

U.S. Department of Homeland Security
Washington, D.C. 20528
Web site: http://www.dhs.gov

World Health Organization (WHO)
Avenue Appia 20
1211 Geneva 27
Switzerland
(+ 41 22) 791 21 11
Web site: http://www.who.int

WEB SITES

Due to the changing nature of Internet links, the Rosen Publishing Group, Inc., has developed an online list of Web sites related to the subject of this book. This site is updated regularly. Please use this link to access the list:

http://www.rosenlinks.com/lwmd/cbwpw

[FOR FURTHER READING]

Haugen, David M. *Biological and Chemical Weapons* (At Issue). San Diego: Greenhaven Press, 2001.

Levine, Herbert M. *Chemical and Biological Weapons in Our Times* (Social Studies: Current Events). London: Franklin Watts, Inc., 2000.

Payan, Gregory. *Chemical and Biological Weapons: Anthrax and Sarin* (High-Tech Military Weapons). New York: Children's Press, 2000.

Pringle, Laurence P. *Chemical and Biological Warfare: The Cruelest Weapons* (Issues in Focus). Berkeley Heights, NJ: Enslow Publishers, 2000.

[BIBLIOGRAPHY]

Alibek, Ken, with Stephen Handelman. *Biohazard: The Chilling True Story of the Largest Covert Biological Weapons Program in the World—Told from Inside by the Man Who Ran It*. New York: Random House, Inc., 1999.

Axtman, Kris. "Campus Labs Eyed After Anthrax Scare." *Christian Science Monitor* online. Accessed June 8, 2004 (http://www.csmonitor.com/2001/1210/p1s3-ussc.html).

Barenblatt, Daniel. *A Plague upon Humanity: The Secret Genocide of Axis Japan's Germ Warfare Operation*. New York: HarperCollins Publishers, Inc., 2004.

Bellamy, Patrick. "False Prophet: The Aum Cult of Terror." CrimeLibrary.com. Accessed April 18, 2004 (http://www.crimelibrary.com/terrorists_spies/terrorists/prophet/1.html?sect=22).

"Biological Weapons." The Environmental Literacy Council. Accessed April 18, 2004 (http://www.enviroliteracy.org/article.php/592.html).

"Bioterrorism and the Use of Anthrax in World War I." University of Georgia College of Veterinary Medicine. Accessed April 18, 2004 (http://www.vet.uga.edu/vpp/IVM/ENG/Modes/anthrax.htm).

Blumenthal, Ralph. "World War II Atrocities: Comparing the Unspeakable to the Unthinkable." *New York Times*. March 7, 1999.

"Century of Biological and Chemical Weapons." September 25, 2001. BBC News Online. Accessed April 18, 2004 (http://news.bbc.co.uk/1/low/world/americas/1562534.stm).

"Chemical and Biological Warfare." The Warfighters Encyclopedia: A Consolidated Ready Reference to U.S. Military History, Traditions, Weapons and Weapons Systems. Accessed April 18,

2004 (http://wrc.chinalake.navy.mil/warfighter_enc/weapons/ chembio/bioagts.htm).

CNN.com: "President Signs Vaccine Legislation." Accessed July 21, 2004 (http://www.cnn.com/2004/ALLPOLITICS/07/21/ bush.vaccine.ap).

"The CQ Researcher: Chemical and Biological Weapons." The CQ Press online. January 31, 1997 issue of *The CQ Researcher*, Volume 7, No. 4, p. 85. Accessed April 18, 2004 (http:// www.cqpress.com/context/articles/cqr_chemical_chronology.html).

Crone, Hugh D. *Banning Chemical Weapons: The Scientific Background*. New York: Cambridge University Press, 1992.

"Emergencies and Disasters: Planning & Prevention." Department of Homeland Security Web site. Accessed April 18, 2004 (http:// www.dhs.gov/dhspublic/display?theme=14&content=462).

Goldberg, Jeffrey. "The Great Terror." *The New Yorker* online. Accessed April 18, 2004 (http://newyorker.com/fact/content/ ?020325fa_FACT1).

Hayes, Laura. "Al Qaeda: Osama bin Laden's Network of Terror." Infoplease.com. Accessed June 8, 2004 (http://www.infoplease.com/ spot/terror-qaeda.html).

"Howard T. Ricketts." Britannica Concise Encyclopedia. 2004. Encyclopædia Britannica. Accessed April 18, 2004 (http:// concise.britannica.com/ebc/article?eu=402212).

Lewis, Susan K. "History of Biowarfare." PBS.org. Accessed April 18, 2004 (http://www.pbs.org/wgbh/nova/bioterror/history.html).

"Louis Pasteur." Wikipedia.org. Accessed April 18, 2004 (http://en.wikipedia.org/wiki/Pasteur).

Mayor, Adrienne. *Greek Fire, Poison Arrows, and Scorpion Bombs: Biological and Chemical Weapons in the Ancient World*. New York: The Overlook Press, Peter Mayer Publishers, Inc., 2003.

Miller, Judith, Stephen Engelberg, and William Broad. *Germs: Biological Weapons and America's Secret War*. New York: Simon & Schuster, 2001.

Olson, Kyle B. "Aum Shinrikyo: Once and Future Threat?" CDC.gov Web site. Accessed April 18, 2004 (http://www.cdc.gov/ncidod/EID/vol5no4/olson.htm).

Onishi, Norimitsu. "Ex-Leader of Japan Cult Sentenced to Death in Gas Attack." Nytimes.com, February 27, 2004. Accessed February 29, 2004 (http://www.nytimes.com/2004/02/27/international/asia/27CNDJAPA.html?ex=1078898919&ei=1&en=eede002db8aba4e0).

"Real Live Killers: Biological Weapons." The Why Files. Accessed April 18, 2004 (http://whyfiles.org/059bio_war/history.html).

Romano, Amy. *Germ Warfare* (The Library of Disease-Causing Organisms). New York: The Rosen Publishing Group, Inc., 2004.

"The Subcommittee on Coast Guard and Maritime Transportation Hearing on Port Security: Shipping Containers." Accessed June 8, 2004 (http://www.house.gov/transportation/cgmt/03-13-02/03-13-02memo.html).

INDEX

ABOUT THE AUTHOR

Janell Broyles is a writer and editor who lives in Brooklyn. This is her third book for the Rosen Publishing Group.

PHOTO CREDITS

Cover © Scott Olson/Getty Images; pp. 4–5 © David McNew/Getty Images; p. 6 © Gilles Peress/Magnum Photos; pp. 8, 20–21, 22, 36 © AP/Wide World Photos; p. 10 © SuperStock; p. 12 (top) © CNRI/Science Photo Library, (bottom) © Eye of Science/Science Photo Library; p. 15 © Toru Yamanaka/AFP/Getty Images; p. 17 © US Army/AP/Wide World Photos; p. 18 ©East News/Getty Images; p. 19 © Alex Wong/Getty Images; p. 23 © FBI/Getty Images; p. 26 © Reuters/Corbis; pp. 28, 29, 35 (inset) © Hulton/Archive/Getty Images; p. 30 Photos12.com/Polaris; pp. 31, 34–35 © Bettmann/Corbis; p. 38 © Marco Di Lauro/Getty Images; p. 39 Ozturk Ramazan/Sipa; p. 41 © Jordan TV/EPA/AP/Wide World Photos; pp. 42–43 © Fujifotos/The Image Works; p. 43 (inset) Kyodo News; p. 45 © D. Sprague/L.A. Daily News/Corbis Sygma; p. 46 © Timothy A. Clary/AFP/Getty Images; p. 48 © UPI/Landov; p. 51 © Chien-Chi Chang/Magnum Photos; p. 52 (top) © Ron Sanford/Corbis, (bottom) © Mark Wilson/Getty Images; p. 54 © Joe Raedle/Getty Images.

Designer: Evelyn Horovicz; Editor: Leigh Ann Cobb; Layout: Thomas Forget; Photo Researcher: Amy Feinberg